What Makes the Sky Blue?

by Janet Slingerland

The Child's World

childsworld.com

Published by The Child's World®
1980 Lookout Drive • Mankato, MN 56003-1705
800-599-READ • www.childsworld.com

Acknowledgments
The Child's World®: Mary Swensen, Publishing Director
Red Line Editorial: Editorial direction and production
The Design Lab: Design

Photographs ©: Shutterstock Images, cover, 1, 5, 9, 15, 19, 21;
NASA/JSC Gateway to Astronaut Photography of Earth, 6; Red
Line Editorial, 10, 16; NASA, 12-13

ISBN 9781503807969
LCCN 2015958151

Printed in the United States of America
Mankato, MN
June, 2016
PA02299

ABOUT THE AUTHOR

Janet Slingerland is a writer, a scout leader, and an engineer. She loves books, science, and books about science. She lives in New Jersey with her husband and three children.

TABLE of CONTENTS

CHAPTER 1

What Is the Atmosphere?

The atmosphere is like a giant bubble surrounding Earth. The bubble is filled with air. This is the atmosphere.

Air looks clear. It has no taste. It does not smell. Yet air is mostly made of gas. There are many gases in air. Nitrogen and oxygen are the most common. There are other gases, too.

But air is not just made of gases. Air has water and dust in it. Sometimes the water is a gas. This is called water vapor. Sometimes there are drops of liquid water in the air.

The air you breathe is mostly nitrogen and oxygen.

The atmosphere looks blue from Earth.
It looks blue from space, too.

Gases in the air are made up of tiny pieces. Each tiny piece is called a **molecule**. Water drops are bigger. So are specks of dust. They are still tiny. They are so small you can't see them.

Look at the sky. You are looking at the atmosphere. Beyond the atmosphere is outer space. Space is mostly empty. There are very few molecules in it. Look at Earth from space. There is a blue haze around the world. This is the atmosphere.

CHAPTER 2

What Is Sunlight?

The sun gives off energy. You feel it as heat. You see it as sunlight. And it travels in waves.

Shake a string up and down quickly. This makes waves. They look like a line of hills. This is what light waves look like.

Waves have wavelengths. A wavelength is the distance between the top of one hill and the top of the next. Light wavelengths are tiny. They are smaller than a piece of sand. They are smaller than a bit of dust.

Light from the sun looks white. But it is really made up of many different colors! Color is **visible** light that reaches your eyes. We see six basic colors: red, orange, yellow, green, blue, and violet. Each color has a different wavelength. The colors

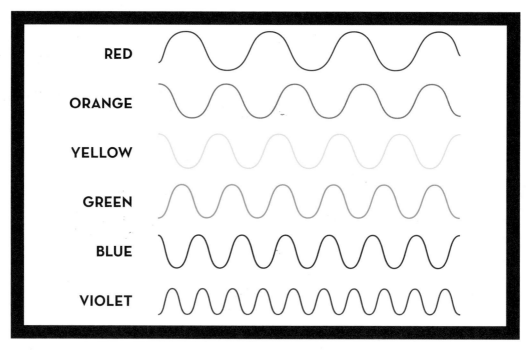

The six basic colors have different wavelengths.

with the shortest wavelengths are blue and violet. Red light has the longest.

You need light to see things. Sunlight shines on everything around you. Light waves hit objects and bounce off them. Then the light waves go into your eyes. The light waves that reach your eyes no longer look white. That is because objects take in some colors of light. They reflect others.

Look at an object near you. It appears to have a color. This is the color of light it reflects. The green grass reflects green light. A red apple reflects red light. A black object reflects no light.

CHAPTER 3

What Makes the Sky Blue?

White sunlight spreads out from the sun. It travels through the emptiness of outer space. White sunlight reaches Earth. It enters the atmosphere. It runs into gas molecules. When sunlight hits the gas molecules,

Sunlight looks white when it enters Earth's atmosphere.

some of the light waves **scatter.** They split off. They bounce around in different directions.

Nitrogen molecules and oxygen molecules are tiny. They are much smaller than light wavelengths. These molecules cause each color of light to scatter differently. Colors with shorter wavelengths scatter more. Colors with longer wavelengths scatter less.

Blue and violet light have short wavelengths. They scatter a lot. Red and orange light have longer wavelengths. They do not scatter as much.

Sometimes the sky looks dark blue.
Other times it looks light blue.

Look up in the sky. Blue light is scattering. The blue light waves are bouncing around. Blue light bounces into your eyes. That is why the sky looks blue!

But the sun is not always over your head. Sometimes it is on the **horizon**. This happens at sunrise and sunset.

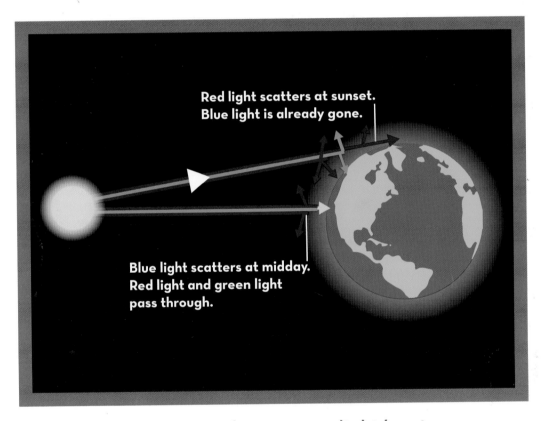

Red light scatters at sunset.
Blue light is already gone.

Blue light scatters at midday.
Red light and green light
pass through.

*At sunrise and sunset, sunlight has to
go through more atmosphere.*

Look at the sunset. The sun is not right over your head. The sun is at a sharp angle. Sunlight has to go through a lot of air now. Most of the blue light scatters before it reaches you. The light left is red and orange. You see a red and orange sky.

This is called Rayleigh scattering. It happens when light meets molecules that are smaller than light wavelengths. It happens when sunlight hits gas molecules in the atmosphere.

CHAPTER 4

Why Are Clouds White?

Dust floats in the air. Water vapor does, too. When the water vapor cools, water drops form on the dust. This is a cloud **particle.**

Sunlight hits the particles. The light scatters. But cloud particles are bigger than gas molecules. They do not scatter light the same way gas molecules do.

Cloud particles scatter all colors in sunlight the same. Red light waves scatter just as much as blue light waves. All colors bounce around equally.

Clouds come in all shapes and sizes.

This is Mie scattering. It happens when light meets particles about the same size as light wavelengths. It happens when sunlight encounters cloud particles.

Look up at a cloud. The light going into your eyes is many colors. The cloud looks white.

Sometimes a cloud is thick. Tiny water droplets combine to make bigger drops. Sunlight hits the cloud. The light scatters away. Little light passes through. The cloud looks gray.

It is day. The sun is high in the sky. Rayleigh scattering happens. You see blue sky. Mie scattering happens. You see white clouds.

It is sunset. Sunlight passes through a lot of air. Rayleigh scattering happens. Blue and green light scatter away. The light reaches you. The sky looks red and orange.

Some sunsets are brighter than others.

Mie scattering happens. The light bounces off the clouds. The clouds look red and orange.

Blue Sky in a Glass

Check out blue light scattering in your own kitchen.

What You Need
tall, clear glass
water
milk
flashlight

What to Do
1. Pour 12 ounces (1 ½ cups) water into the glass. Mix in ¼ teaspoon milk.
2. Shine a light through the back of the glass. The light looks white. Not much has scattered.
3. Shine the light down into the glass. The milk particles are scattering the blue light.
4. Add another ¼ teaspoon milk. Shine the light at the side of the glass. Look at the water. It looks blue. You see the blue light scattering.
5. Shine the light through the back of the glass. The light looks yellow or orange.

Glossary

horizon (hu-RY-zuhn) The horizon is the line where the land or sea seems to meet the sky. The sun rises and sets on the horizon.

molecule (MOL-uh-kyool) A molecule is the smallest piece of a substance that can exist. A gas molecule is so small you cannot see it.

particle (PAHR-tuh-kuhl) A particle is a very small piece of something. A cloud particle is made up of a water droplet and a tiny speck of dust.

scatter (SKAT-er) When objects scatter, they go in many different directions. Molecules in the air cause light waves to scatter.

visible (VIZ-uh-buhl) An object is visible when it can be seen. Trees are visible in the sunlight.

To Learn More

In the Library

Bennett, Jeffrey. *Max Goes to Mars: A Science Adventure with Max the Dog.* Chicago: Big Kid Science, 2015.

Johnson, Robin. *What Are Light Waves?* New York: Crabtree, 2014.

Pfeffer, Wendy. *Light Is All around Us.* New York: HarperCollins, 2014.

On the Web

Visit our Web site for links about the sky: **childsworld.com/links**

Note to Parents, Teachers, and Librarians: We routinely verify our Web links to make sure they are safe and active sites. So encourage your readers to check them out!

Index